0102157

P9-DDZ-290

ON LINE

JBIOG
Lange
Venezia, Mike

Dorothea Lange

GETTING TO KNOW THE WORLD'S GREATEST ARTISTS

DOROTHEA
LANGE

WRITTEN AND ILLUSTRATED BY MIKE VENEZIA

CHILDREN'S PRESS®
A DIVISION OF GROLIER PUBLISHING
NEW YORK   LONDON   HONG KONG   SYDNEY
DANBURY, CONNECTICUT

Cover: *Migrant Mother,* by Dorothea Lange. 1936. Photograph. © the Dorothea Lange Collection, The Oakland Museum of California, City of Oakland. Gift of Paul S. Taylor.

Colorist for illustrations: Kathy Hickey

Library of Congress Cataloging-in-Publication Data

Venezia, Mike.
  Dorothea Lange / written and illustrated by Mike Venezia.
    p. cm. — (Getting to know the world's greatest artists)
   Summary: Discusses the life and work of the twentieth century American photographer Dorothea Lange.
  ISBN 0-516-22026-8 (lib.bdg.)   0-516-27171-7 (pbk.)
   1. Lange, Dorothea—Juvenile literature. 2. Women photographers—United States—Biography—Juvenile literature. 3. Photographers—United States—Biography—Juvenile literature. [1. Lange, Dorothea. 2. Photographers. 3. Women Biography.] I. Title.
  TR140.L3 V46 2000
  770'.92—dc21   99-058034
                                                  CIP
                                                  AC

Visit Children's Press on the Internet at:
http://publishing.grolier.com

GROLIER
PUBLISHING

Copyright 2000 by Mike Venezia.
All rights reserved. Published simultaneously in Canada.
Printed in the United States of America.
1 2 3 4 5 6 7 8 9 10 R 09 08 07 06 05 04 03 02 01 00

Portrait of Dorothea Lange, by Paul S. Taylor. 1934. Photograph. © the Dorothea Lange Collection, The Oakland Museum of California, City of Oakland. Gift of Paul S. Taylor.

Dorothea Lange was born in 1895 in Hoboken, New Jersey. She lived during one of the unhappiest times in American history—the Great Depression. Dorothea's photographs from that period are some of the best-known and most powerful pictures of the twentieth century.

The Great Depression began in 1929 and lasted for more than ten years. No one had any idea it was coming or how it would change their lives. It was a time when, almost overnight, millions of people in the United States lost their savings, jobs, and homes.

Part of the reason it happened was that too many people borrowed and invested their money unwisely. When it was time to pay the money back, people found they didn't have enough. Families sometimes had to sell their houses, farms, and cars. Since no one had very much money to spend, many factories and stores closed too, and things kept getting worse.

Drought Refugees from Oklahoma, by Dorothea Lange. 1935. Photograph. © the Dorothea Lange Collection, The Oakland Museum of California, City of Oakland. Gift of Paul S. Taylor.

Dorothea Lange's best-known photographs show the people and families who were affected most by the Great Depression. Dorothea had a way of picturing people in a caring, sensitive way that had rarely been seen before.

Damaged Child, by Dorothea Lange. Photograph. © the Dorothea Lange Collection, The Oakland Museum of California, City of Oakland. Gift of Paul S. Taylor.

Man Beside Wheelbarrow, by Dorothea Lange. 1934. Photograph. © the Dorothea Lange Collection, The Oakland Museum of California, City of Oakland. Gift of Paul S. Taylor.

Hoe Culture, by Dorothea Lange. 1936. Photograph. © the Dorothea Lange Collection, The Oakland Museum of California, City of Oakland. Gift of Paul S. Taylor.

Dorothea didn't even have to photograph people's faces to show the suffering and loneliness many people felt at this time.

Dorothea Lange grew up in a nice neighborhood in Hoboken. When she was six years old, she caught a serious disease called polio. Today polio can be prevented, but in Dorothea's time it disabled many children. Dorothea's right leg and foot were badly damaged and she walked with a limp for the rest of her life.

Lange's Birthplace, by Dorothea Lange. Photograph. © the Dorothea Lange Collection, The Oakland Museum of California, City of Oakland. Gift of Paul S. Taylor.

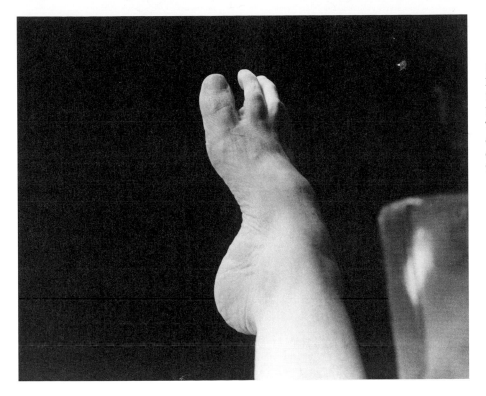

Dorothea could no longer run and jump like she had before. Some kids even made fun of her. Dorothea grew up feeling angry, sad, and embarrassed all at the same time.

When she became a photographer, Dorothea took a picture of her right foot. She said her damaged foot was the most important thing that ever happened to her. Because of her foot, she always worked hard not to let her problems get her down, and that made her a stronger, more understanding person.

Lower East Side in New York City Around the Turn of the Century, 1914. Photograph. Photographer unknown.
© Corbis-Bettmann.

Dorothea went to school in New York City, which was right across the Hudson River from Hoboken. Her mother worked as a librarian there. New York was much different from her own quiet neighborhood. It was crowded and exciting. Dorothea loved to study the interesting people she saw every day.

Sometimes, when she went to meet her mother after school, Dorothea had to walk through dangerous neighborhoods. Since she couldn't run fast, she invented a way to give herself a blank expression so that no one would notice her. She called it her "cloak of invisibility." Later, Dorothea used her "cloak" to study people without them knowing she was even around.

When Dorothea graduated from high school, she surprised everyone by announcing she wanted to be a photographer. Dorothea had never owned a camera or even taken a picture, but with her great imagination and interest in people, Dorothea knew she'd do just fine.

She started out by convincing a well-known New York portrait photographer to give her a job as an assistant. It wasn't long before Dorothea learned how to use a camera, develop film, make prints, and run a studio.

San Francisco Street Scene. Photograph. Photographer unknown. © Corbis-Bettmann.

After getting her confidence up, Dorothea decided to travel around the world to learn more about people and practice her photography. When she was twenty-two years old, Dorothea left New York with her best girl friend. They made it only as far as San Francisco, California, though, because a pickpocket stole all their money. Dorothea ended up staying in San Francisco.

She got a job right away in a department store and joined a camera club. Dorothea met and became friends with lots of photographers and artists. One of those friends offered to lend Dorothea enough money to start up her own portrait studio.

Dorothea was thrilled to have the chance to run her own business. She soon became very successful making unusual portraits of wealthy mothers and their children.

Dorothea invited her friends to come over to her new studio every day after work. They enjoyed discussing the latest things happening in art and photography and listening to new jazz music on the phonograph.

Home Of The Desert Rat, by Maynard Dixon. 1944-45. Oil on canvas, mounted on masonite.
Bequest of Leon H. Woolsey. Photograph by Craig Smith. © Phoenix Art Museum.

One of Dorothea's guests was the well-known western painter Maynard Dixon. Dorothea enjoyed Maynard's company. He dressed like a cowboy and had all kinds of exciting stories to tell. Maynard and Dorothea fell in love, and got married in 1922.

Maynard and Dorothea had two sons, John and Dan. Even though Maynard was a loving father and husband, he often spent weeks and even months away from his family. While he was off painting pictures of deserts and mountains, Dorothea was left at home raising the boys, taking care of the house, and running the portrait studio.

Maynard and Dan Painting, by Dorothea Lange. 1920s. Photograph. © the Dorothea Lange Collection, The Oakland Museum of California, City of Oakland. Gift of Paul S. Taylor.

After years of doing this, Dorothea and Maynard finally agreed that their marriage wasn't working very well. They decided to live apart from each other. In 1929, they sent their sons to a boarding school and rented separate studios.

Man Eating at White Angel Bread Line, by Dorothea Lange. 1933. Photograph. © the Dorothea Lange Collection, The Oakland Museum of California, City of Oakland. Gift of Paul S. Taylor.

In 1933, during one of the worst years of the Depression, Dorothea noticed from her studio window dozens of men who were out of work. They were standing in a breadline waiting for a free meal.

She decided to go out and photograph them. One of the pictures she brought back was called *White Angel Bread Line*. Dorothea put a print of it up on the wall of her studio.

When her friends asked her what she was going to do with photographs of starving homeless people, Dorothea told them she had no idea. All Dorothea knew was that she had to take more pictures to show what a serious problem the Great Depression was.

White Angel Bread Line, by Dorothea Lange. 1933. Photograph. © the Dorothea Lange Collection, The Oakland Museum of California, City of Oakland. Gift of Paul S. Taylor.

Dorothea spent more and more time outside her comfortable studio. She often went to dangerous areas to photograph people who were tired and sometimes angry. This is when her cloak of invisibility really came in handy.

General Strike - Policeman, by Dorothea Lange. 1934. Photograph. © the Dorothea Lange Collection, The Oakland Museum of California, City of Oakland. Gift of Paul S. Taylor.

One day, a friend suggested that Dorothea have a show of all the remarkable photographs she had been taking. In 1934, Dorothea had her first show at a small California gallery.

At this exhibit, Dorothea's photographs could be seen for the first time by lots of people. One person who went to the show thought Dorothea's pictures would be perfect to go along with some articles he was writing. Paul Taylor was a college professor who was studying the problems people were having because of the Great Depression.

Ditched, Stalled, and Stranded, by Dorothea Lange. 1936. Photograph. © the Dorothea Lange Collection, The Oakland Museum of California, City of Oakland. Gift of Paul S. Taylor.

Paul asked Dorothea if he could use one of her photographs for a government report he was writing. He then asked her if she would go along and work with him. Dorothea agreed. She couldn't wait to begin using her skills to help record the Great Depression.

Untitled (Migrant Housing, CA), by Dorothea Lange. 1936. Photograph. © the Dorothea Lange Collection, The Oakland Museum of California, City of Oakland. Gift of Paul S. Taylor.

Dorothea and Paul made a great team. They worked hard gathering information from many of the thousands of migrant families who arrived in California every day.

Most migrants were ordinary people who had lost their farms and homes. They traveled all over the country hoping to get jobs picking fruit, vegetables, or cotton. They were so poor that they often had to live in old tents or cardboard boxes without heat, running water, or much food.

Dorothea took a picture of the migrant mother below. In it you can almost feel how worried that mother was about her children's future and where they would get their next meal. This picture became one of the most famous photographs of the Great Depression.

Migrant Mother, by Dorothea Lange. 1936. Photograph. © the Dorothea Lange Collection, The Oakland Museum of California, City of Oakland. Gift of Paul S. Taylor.

Tenant Farmer in Texas to
migrant laborer in California

1927 made $7000
1928 broke even
1929 went in the hole
1930 still deeper
1931 lost everything
1932 hit road

Marysville Camp   August, 1935

Tenant Farmer in Texas to Migrant Laborer in California, by Dorothea Lange. 1935. Photograph. © the Dorothea Lange Collection, The Oakland Museum of California, City of Oakland. Gift of Paul S. Taylor.

Dorothea and Paul sent their reports to Washington, D.C. This information was used by the United States government to convince more fortunate Americans that the migrant families needed help.

Dorothea Lange divorced Maynard Dixon and married

Old Man, Centerville, by Dorothea Lange. 1942. Photograph. © the Dorothea Lange Collection, The Oakland Museum of California, City of Oakland. Gift of Paul S. Taylor.

Two Women and Child in Front of Shack, by Dorothea Lange. 1936. Photograph. ©the Dorothea Lange Collection, The Oakland Museum of California, City of Oakland. Gift of Paul S. Taylor.

Paul Taylor in 1935. She lived to be seventy years old, and spent most of the rest of her life traveling around the country with Paul, photographing people in America who were very poor and were treated unfairly. Dorothea wanted to make sure no one would forget about them.

One of Dorothea's favorite cameras was a big clunky one called a Graflex. She preferred it to smaller cameras because it forced her to take her time and set up her photographs more carefully.

Dorothea's photographs are known as documentary photographs. Their purpose was to record information and facts. But few documentary photographers have ever made pictures that are as artistic and caring as Dorothea Lange's.

Works of art in this book can be seen at the following places:

The Oakland Museum of California, Oakland, California
Phoenix Art Museum, Phoenix, Arizona